100 Ways

TO LIVE A

Luxurious

LIFE ON A BUDGET

FIONA FERRIS

Contents

Dear lovely reader,

Perhaps you desire to live a more luxurious life, but the money isn't *quite* there for it. No, my budget doesn't allow for all those expensive fancy things either, but I do know that you can add luxe touches to your daily life if you so desire. And with no expenditure necessary.

This mini-book is a virtual pick'n'mix of ideas and reminders, and a blend of both mindset and practical suggestions. It is intended as a quick read for you to dip into whenever you need a boost of inspiration. Some of these ideas may not be new to you, but I find it is always helpful to have a refresh.

I have small books like this from other authors and I love to slip one into the side pocket of my handbag, so I have something uplifting to read while I wait somewhere. I simply pick up where I last stopped reading, and when I get to the end, I go back to the beginning. It's a wonderful repeat loop of inspiration that never stops!

Or if the tips are numbered, such as in this book, it's fun to choose a number at random and go to that entry and challenge yourself to implement that point.

I hope you feel the energy in this book and that it inspires and motivates you to live your best life every day. There really is magic when we combine real life with a big imagination. I know because I felt it while I was writing this title.

We do not need to wait for 'one day when' to begin living our dream life. I truly believe we are all here at this time to fully express who we are and to also enjoy ourselves every single day. Even while working, taking care of things at home, and doing all the normal things we need to get done.

Life is too short not to add some sparkle and flair; the details make everything better. We can be an inspiration to others in the way we live *and* get to have fabulous fun at the same time.

Life is good! Life is for the living!

I hope you love this book and get *loads* of useful nuggets from it. Now let's get straight into one-hundred ways you can create your luxurious life... on a budget!

With all my best from beautiful Hawke's Bay, New Zealand,

Fiona

100 Ways to Live a Luxurious Life on a Budget

1. **Find interests you are fully passionate about**. Is it baking? Crafting? Gymnastics? Floral arrangements? Tennis? Think about what you enjoyed doing as a little girl and revisit some of those activities, maybe in the same way, or perhaps the grown-up version. When you look forward to getting back to something you are working on it elevates your life experience, and you become a more magnetic person too – your enthusiasm makes you sparkle. Writing is one of those things for me. When I am writing a new book I get *so enthused* about everything, and life feels wonderful. It's like being lit from within. What are those things for you?

2.   **Create new no-spend rituals** – brunch at home on the weekend, a picnic in the park in summer, cozy movie afternoons in your living room in the winter, dressing up and going for a stroll through a beautiful part of town in the autumn. There are so many activities you can do for zero money. Something I love to do is see how abundant and cosseted I can feel while spending as little as possible, preferably nothing! One example for me is 'going shopping' at our local library to borrow the latest issue of a favourite magazine and a few 'new' books. Note down your favourites so you remember them again for the future. Develop a bank of beautiful rituals to sustain you as you build your financial wealth. Spending money isn't the only way to have fun, and you get to increase your capacity for creativity as well.

3.   **Love living below your means**. Struggling to pay your bills or lying awake at night stressing over your ever-increasing debt is *not* a luxurious lifestyle. The feeling of luxury shouldn't only be reserved for rich people either though. The media tells us what a 'luxury lifestyle' is supposed to look like. But we get to decide that for ourselves. By not just blindly following trends and fads and living within the money we have, we can welcome the feelings of being carefree, unburdened, light-as-air, prosperous, wealthy and content. See

living within your means as *the key* to living a luxurious life, not a hindrance to one.

4. **Develop a luxury mindset**. Work on expanding your definition of luxury from mere possessions to coveting the *feeling* of luxury in all aspects of your life. As well, infuse your mindset with a happy thriftiness where you milk every drop of enjoyment from money spent. Peruse online inspiration and soak it in, but also be discerning. Quality doesn't always have to come with a crazy price tag; often pricing is used as a marketing tool. A luxury lifestyle is having money in the bank and investments for your future, not just material goods you may not like or even remember six months later.

5. **Brainstorm creative ways you can live more luxuriously** on your current budget. Research ideas online and from books and note down any that appeal. Dream up your own too. Dedicate a notebook to your luxurious living ideas. For me the first thought that comes to mind is having unlimited relaxing time – living lavishly without spending extra money means reading a book with my feet up and a cup of tea. The second thought is using my lovely perfumes every day. We all have items around our home that we just don't use – we save them for a special day.

But if we'd just use those things, we can make every day special. Don't buy the thin, cheap body lotion, luxuriate in the body cream you were given for Christmas two years ago!

6. **Feel luxuriously elegant** by tidying and cleaning your home extra well. Look around you and see how you can transform your home to feel more sumptuous. Keep in mind the vibe of a five-star hotel as you go. Style your home as if it were a high-end Air BnB waiting for its first guest. Neatly stack a small selection of appealing magazines (it doesn't matter if they aren't current – I keep some favourite magazines from years ago for re-reading). Light a candle, perhaps a tea-light in a pretty glass or a scented candle you received as a gift that you've never lit. Play sultry music you'd imagine hearing in a cool hotel lobby. Put fresh flowers in a bud vase on the bathroom vanity, or by the sink in your kitchen. Even in a basic garden there is almost always something flowering, or perhaps you will snip off a few sprigs of rosemary or a tiny spray of leaves. I imagine a rich lady pottering around doing this; why not us too!

7. **Wear your better clothes** when you are doing ordinary errands. Not a ball dress of course, but you will have slightly nicer items that you keep for special. Wear that dressy top

with your jeans and feel high vibe having a coffee with your friend. People are so casual these days that you can really stand out as someone with style – and wealth – without making a lot of effort at all. Sometimes when I have worn something nicer than I normally would I have people ask me, 'Are you from around here?' which I take as a total compliment!

8. **Be a tourist in your town**. No matter where you live, I can guarantee there will be reasons for tourists to visit. But do you ever appreciate these? If you're anything like me, the answer is a big no! In Napier, the town where I live, people visit from all over the world to see the beautiful Art Deco buildings. Napier was near levelled by a huge earthquake in 1931, so the resulting rebuild meant all the buildings were constructed in a similar Art Deco style of the era. There are walking tours in the summer; I often see small groups being led around by a guide. I have this city right on my doorstep to view any time I like. What do you have that you can enjoy?

9. **Go on vacation tonight**. On YouTube there are walking tours of virtually anywhere you would care to 'visit'. And if you have a television that can access YouTube you can view a walking tour on the big screen. Last

night my husband and I 'walked around' a huge mall in London, then took a tour of the Plaza Hotel in NYC, and finished off our evening with a walking tour of the streets of Florence in Italy, even popping into some of the local churches. We really felt like we had been on a little trip! My best tip is to mute the sound and play complementary music with your tour instead of the commentary.

10. **Read a novel set amongst the glittering rich**. It is such fun to become engrossed in a book set in a fabulous location with wealthy characters. *Queen Bee* by Jane Fallon is focused on wealthy sorts living in a well-to-do English enclave, and describes behind-the-scenes details of their glamorous lives. (Of course, nothing is as it seems, but that's the fun too). And Penny Vincenzi books are glorious also – she writes within the moneyed London set. I can feel like I'm part of their world as I enjoy one of her books. In fact, immersing myself in this borrowed wealth elevates my thinking and makes me want to live better – more fresh salads and less frozen pizza!

11. **Watch stylish movies**. In the same vein it's fun to watch movies or a television series where the setting is rich and stylish. Movies like *The Devil Wears Prada*, and newer series

such as *Riviera* and *Inventing Anna* never fail to help me up my game effortlessly. My personal standards rise, I dress better, and even my posture improves. Nancy Meyers movies are great for this too, and don't forget old movies such as *To Catch a Thief* and *Breakfast at Tiffany's* – they are *so* elegant and inspiring. Keep a running list of movies and television shows that help you feel motivated and like the next-level you. Administer doses as necessary!

12. **Take extra care with your hair and makeup**. I used to wear no makeup if I planned not to leave the house that day, but now I put on a little makeup every morning. I enjoy the process of doing it, plus it enhances my looks. It's the same with my hair; I would do the bare minimum or just tie it up, but now I do it in the morning so it looks nice all day. When you do your hair and makeup as early as you can, you can then forget about it. It's a small investment of time that has a fabulous payoff because you feel better about yourself, and you don't have a panic if someone calls in or you have to pop out. You might not wear makeup at all and be happy with that. All I'm saying is to decide what makes you feel good and do that, then you're sorted for the day.

13. **Choose to live well no matter your income**. Have impeccable manners, and listen to people, giving them your full attention. Hold beautiful posture. Keep immaculate hygiene. Clear clutter from your home and keep it neat. Talk kindly to anyone you encounter. Be a person of your word. Choose to see the good in people. Cultivate a positive mindset. Avoid the news and read a book instead. Prioritize sleep and try to get eight hours a night. Hydrate your body by sipping water often. All these things cost nothing yet add up to a dignified, elegant, and happy life experience.

14. **Instead of yet more online shopping** (yes, I'm guilty of this myself – the pictures always look so good!) organize your wardrobe instead. Reacquaint yourself with what you already own. Create an enticing 21-piece capsule wardrobe for the next month (as detailed in Chapter 5 of my book *The Chic Closet*). Put on probation (or donate straight away) clothes that make you feel drab or frumpy. See how good your wardrobe looks *without* those clothes hanging there. It's incredible how it works, but when you do this, you will feel like you have more choices rather than less. It's like magic!

15. **Cultivate your 'rich girl' look** from pieces you already own along with ideas from Pinterest. Take the time to blow-dry your hair. Wear your big sunglasses and scarves. Your rich girl style will be different to mine, but for me I like classic pieces with a touch of boho, gold jewellery whether costume or real, and soft-bright shades such as tomato red, daffodil yellow or grass green tops paired with neutral bottoms – white jeans, light blue jeans, and black jeans or trousers. Shoes make all the difference, and heels with jeans always feel chic to me. What is your rich girl look?

16. **Clean = luxurious**. Clean your jewellery until it sparkles – dish soap and hot water is great for most things except delicate items such as pearls and emeralds. Ensure all your clothing is clean, and ironed or steamed. Get rid of anything that has an unrepairable hole (unless intentional such as ripped jeans) or unmoveable stains. Wash your makeup brushes and clean all your makeup compacts inside and out (use a tiny amount of your least-favourite perfume or isopropyl alcohol on a clean rag). Wipe around the neck of your nail polish bottles with nail polish remover on a cotton ball. All these little details will make your items feel *brand new*.

17.   **Look after your clothes**. Wash them gently and iron straight away if pressing is needed. Snip loose threads. Sew on any loose buttons. Pull snags through to the back with a tiny crochet hook. Unpick or snip off scratchy labels. Hang all your current season clothes up rather than have items stuffed in a drawer. Space out the hangers. Merchandise your closet so that it looks as appealing as a boutique! Polish your shoes. Check the heels and soles and have them repaired if you feel they are worth the cost of doing this. Having everything you own be ready to wear is *such* a luxury feeling.

18.   **Go for a walk near water**. Where I live we have a beachfront in the city. Dressing casual but nice, with big sunglasses and a pair of stylish walking shoes feels like I'm on vacation, and all for the cost of some petrol to get there. I know petrol is priced almost like gold these days, but it's still an inexpensive getaway, and if you really want to go all out, have an ice cream or coffee too! Is there a beach walk or lake near you? Or what about a public park or botanical garden? Getting out into nature is one of the best ways to feel 'rich'.

19.   **Browse in expensive boutiques** or home stores, *just to see*. Just to see the styles and colours used, the sumptuous textures, and

elegant scents. I am always inspired when I do this, and I don't have to spend a cent to be so. I get new ideas and change things up when I get home, whether it's in my closet or my living room. I saw some beautiful leopard print cushions at a design store, and they were $450 for two cushions. I know! I didn't want to spend that, so I bought a piece of leopard print fabric for less than $20 and made two square covers on my sewing machine.

20. **Look to others who live a good life** and see what they do that is different to you. If it is someone in the media, take note of their clothing style and how they dress to express themselves. Borrow some of their ideas for yourself. When I used to read tabloid magazines I loved to see what the stars were wearing as they walked through airports. It wasn't hard to adopt that big sunglasses-stylish tote bag-giant looped scarf look for myself. If it's someone in your real life, observe their habits. I have been inspired personally by wealthy couples we have met – they are warm, welcoming and generous, not only with money, but with a generosity of spirit. These are qualities anyone can cultivate.

21. **Be friends with money**. Many people are intimidated by money and finance. I know because I used to be nervous of it too. Then I

changed my mindset to think of it as fun and exciting. I started to love checking in with my bank accounts each week and keeping my financial admin tidy. I read stories online of people who had gotten ahead by living simply but elegantly. I adopted that for myself and it became a fun game to see how well my husband and I could live while saving for our first home. (See my book *Financially Chic* for all the details on how we paid that home off early too, I share everything we did.)

22. **Only keep items that are clean and functional**. Ensure that anything you surround yourself with is in good repair. You cannot feel rich when you have dirty, broken things around. Do what you need to do. Clean them up, repair if possible, or replace if you must when you can. I have found this makes a *huge* difference to how good I feel. If a glass is chipped, I'll throw it out, even if it was expensive. It does not feel high vibe to drink from a chipped glass! Likewise with items you use every day – polish your kettle and wipe down your toaster. Clean the light switches and door handles. Replace burnt out light bulbs. These are all small things but they do make a difference.

23. **Change your environment to change your life**. You won't believe the huge difference this makes until you try it. Moving pictures or small furniture pieces to a different area, swapping decorative pillows between beds and sofas, having only a few décor items displayed on the sideboard or occasional tables and rotating them regularly, using different dinner sets if you have more than one, changing bedding colours if you have multiple bedspreads or duvet covers, and shifting potted plants (indoor or outdoor) to other parts of the house or garden. There is no end to how you can make things appear fresh and new when you see them in a different spot. My husband Paul always likes things 'the same', so I do this when he is out. But when he gets home he raves about how good things look!

24. **Educate yourself on topics that interest you**. Don't be that person who only scrolls social media for entertainment. Decide on something you've always wanted to learn about and do that instead, or at least as well as. Watch YouTube videos on art history. Learn flower arranging from a library book. Perfect your macaron technique from a website recipe. Take a wine appreciation course. Be rich in your mind, and surprise people with your enthusiasm for a topic. Most people when you

ask them 'what they've been up to lately' will answer with the latest television show they're watching or the fact that work is busy. But you are not most people! You can say that you have been studying the renaissance painters and how fascinating their background stories are. Now *that* is living well.

25. **Look up free or inexpensive outings to go to**. Art gallery exhibition openings are a great one – you will find fashionable people sipping wine and viewing the art in front of them. It's an outing where you can dress up, have a good time, and meet people. You might even find beautiful new art for your home too. It's a win/win: you will be helping an up-and-coming artist who will be thrilled to have a good turnout at their exhibition. And if you see something you like, they get to sell a piece and have it gone to a home where it is appreciated, plus you could own an original work of art at a great price.

26. **Remember your 'why'** – why are you doing what you are doing? Keep the grand vision you have for your life right in front of you. Your grand vision doesn't need to be big either – my grand vision is to live a simple and peaceful life with plenty of free space around me, both physically and in my schedule. When I 'forget' this, I can get caught up in comparing myself

with others and it ties me up into knots! When I go back to what makes *me* feel abundant and prosperous, I truly do feel like I am living my most luxurious life.

27. **Cut out things that are not so important to you** so you have money available for what is. I know people who *love* their bought coffee – it really is the highlight of their day, and I'm happy for them! I'm not that fussed though and happily make my own coffee, but I do love getting a pedicure. When you identify your 'absolute favourites' vs 'nice to have but wouldn't miss it if I didn'ts', you will find you have more funds available for other things. Work out your priorities so you know what you want to spend your money on. You might start a rainy-day fund with that money, pay off debt, or open a drip-feed investment account.

28. **Keep your vibration high** by doing things that make you feel good – listening to music, moving your body, watching a funny or stylish movie, re-reading a favourite book, journaling inspiring ideas, writing down exciting goals for the next year, re-creating a fashion look from Pinterest, or dressing from your tidied and styled closet. There really are so many ways to feel pleasure daily, and when you do all those little things you really will feel like the most luxurious girl around. Make yourself a list of

all the things *you* enjoy doing and be sure to indulge often.

29. **Become a completer of tasks**. Something I guarantee will make you feel so luxurious and high vibe is to become someone who finishes jobs off properly. When you start doing this it will change your life. You will suddenly feel like you are living your dream life because of the energy freed up. Big and little things such as booking a dentist appointment for a long-overdue check-up, small repair jobs, picking up out-of-place items and putting them away instead of walking past them five times, making your bed first thing in the morning, and doing a job straight away when you see that it needs to be done. Write down a big list of all the little pesky things that are bothering you right now, and commit to ticking them off.

30. **Cook an extra special dinner** on an ordinary weekday. It doesn't need to have expensive ingredients, sometimes I'll just try a new recipe (the simpler the better) which has my husband happily cleaning his plate and me feeling like we have dined at a restaurant even though I was the one who cooked. Cooking with fresh ingredients helps with the 'fancy restaurant' feeling too. When I add more vegetables and have less of the stodgy stuff such as rice or potato, it feels more elegant and

dignified. Somehow I imagine this is how rich people dine! And, amazingly, I am never hungry afterwards even though I have had less food.

31. **Add fresh herbs to your meals**. It's so easy and inexpensive to grow herb plants, and the payback they give you is immense. My favourites for ease of maintenance and yumminess are parsley, thyme and rosemary. You can sprinkle parsley over scrambled eggs, whip it into mashed potato with butter, and mix into a tomato pasta sauce. Thyme is wonderful to zing up a gourmet pizza along with blue cheese and sliced mushroom, mix into a creamy sauce to pour over pan-fried chicken, and to roast potatoes with (I sprinkle pulled-off thyme leaves on an oiled oven tray and place the cut side of a potato on the tiny leaves). Rosemary is beautiful roasted with lamb, chopped finely and layered into a potato gratin, or again, as a roast potato herb option. High-end restaurants use a lot of fresh herbs, so why not make your own restaurant-quality meals at home? Plus, as well as enhancing the deliciousness of a meal, each herb has different health benefits so you will be adding to your rich girl glow at the same time.

32. **Commit to keeping a slim kitchen**. Clean out your pantry and make it your mission to

eat everything before you buy any more groceries. Try not buying groceries for a week except for fresh items as you need them. Have a freezer stocktake – remove everything and, working quickly, note down all items on a pad of paper – guaranteed you will find more than you thought you had. With mystery foods either use them up or throw them out. Doing this feels *so good*. It's wonderful to have a fridge, freezer and pantry that has plenty of space, and all the foods in it you are happy to see.

33. **Make the most of your food budget**. Don't let anything go to waste! Freeze single portions of leftovers for a quick free meal. Label the container with masking tape and a permanent marker so you can find them again. I have had so many delicious lunches this way. My husband might take one to work and heat it in the microwave in the lunchroom. I like to use a non-stick frying pan to heat mine, and if something has a tiny portion that most people might throw away, I keep it, and add a fried egg on the side (cooked in the same pan). *Et voila*, a delicious, healthy, minimal effort, protein-filled, and highly inexpensive lunch.

34. **Work out your ideal supermarket routine**. I played around with stretching out my supermarket shop so that I went once every two weeks or even longer, but then found I dreaded going because my list was so long. I tried grocery delivery too but decided I like to choose my own fresh produce. Now I go every week on a Monday and only stock up on what I need for that week. Combining this regular routine with actively using up what I have in my pantry, fridge and freezer means that my grocery list is quite manageable and not too expensive either. Work out the *easiest* way that you too can fulfil your grocery needs.

35. **Turn your dishwasher on before it's full**. I used to jam-pack our dishwasher and wait to switch it on 'just one more meal, one more meal'. It stressed me out running out of items, *and* it was a big production to unload afterwards. Plus, I don't think our dishes were cleaned so well. I recalled when we were on vacation in a serviced apartment that we would run the dishwasher each day whether it was full or not because there were only a few plates and cups available. Now that I don't try to get use out of every square inch of our dishwasher I get that vacation feeling every day. It's still a full load, it's just not full-full, if you know what I mean. I highly recommend it!

36. **List all the ways in which you live a luxurious life already**. It's like a gratitude list, but better. For me I would list things such as: I get to sleep in on weekends if I want to, I can have a nap on a Sunday afternoon, I live in a quiet country area but get to go to town too, I love the age that I am and the era in which I grew up as well as the time of life I am in right now. I get to decide my daily schedule. I get to write books on the topics I love. Plus, I list the flossier things such as favourite clothing items that make me feel fabulous. Make a list for yourself and aim for one hundred – it might take some time and you'll have to shake everything out of your head that you can, but this exercise will leave you feeling amazing!

37. **Create your own personal brand**. What kind of image would you love to portray to others? When I think about it, mine is approachable and friendly, inclusive, happy, effortless casual chic, down-to-earth, and elegant. It's such an enjoyable thing to think about: firstly, you're dreaming up your most ideal self, then you get to fill in the fun details. What would this lady's home look like? How would she dress? What does she eat? How does she converse with others? How does she entertain? What does the inside of her car look like? Is she an organized and tidy person? Is she good with money? Does she have

confidence in herself? Consider all these aspects and be inspired to be her!

38. **Have high personal standards**. Commit to yourself that you are not just going to accept any old behaviour, either from yourself or others. You can't expect to receive something unless you claim it for yourself first. Imagine if you were the ideal you with your standards raised. Even thinking about having elevated personal standards makes me instantly stand up straighter and be more productive. It seems to me that people who live a luxurious life are generally ones who try harder. They get up earlier, work more diligently, and put more of an effort in. They don't seem to be unhappy about this though, in fact they love being a person who is winning at life. And it all starts with raised personal standards.

39. **Go to a movie at the theatre**. With all the streaming apps available, many of us have fallen out of the habit of going to the cinema. Perhaps that's not a bad thing though, because when you return – and you should! – you will feel wowed all over again from the experience of watching a movie on the big screen. Especially if it is a sumptuous and glamorous affair that moves you, uplifts your mood and your desires, and has you feeling like a new person with different values. How wonderful

that you can be reborn for the price of a movie ticket and a couple of hours of your time!

40. **Live a five-star life**. Decide that you are worthy of living a five-star life, because, well, why not? Journal what belongs in *your* version of a five-star life and start putting into practice what you come up with. Perhaps in your five-star life you'd have a private chef, which may not *quite* be in your budget, but you can be the private chef for yourself. You could wash and chop vegetables a few times a week so you always have beautiful ingredients ready to use at a minute's notice. Or you could come up with a menu of easy, healthy and delicious meals that are your absolute favourites to choose from. You could also make double portions of meals where this is appropriate; for example, spaghetti Bolognese, meatloaf, casserole, lasagne, and put extra portions in the freezer for a ready-made meal. What details belong in your five-star life and how can you bring them into your reality today?

41. **Keep only your good things**. If your linen closet is overflowing, take everything out and put back only the newest, nicest items, donating everything else to a charity store, your local women's refuge or, for the really raggy things, an animal shelter. Do the same with your shoes – pull them all out and put

back only your favourites and most loved. Look at the rest. Are there any that are uncomfortable on your feet or that you just don't want to wear anymore? Bin or donate them, depending on their condition. Do this for each category in your home and feel your energy *transform*.

42. **Use your good things every day**. If you haven't quite gotten around to getting rid of your not-so-good things yet, decide that from today onwards you are going to use your lovely stuff more. The beautiful dishes that only come out once a year, decide that they are your weekend plates. Use your best glasses even though they might get broken. A friend of mine gave me a set of stemmed water goblets that were his late mother's, and they had barely been used. He knew they were my style, and he also knows that I use my nice things. Now when we have dinner at the table, we always use Jean's glasses for sparkling water.

43. **Make a wish list** of things you would like or need, so you have ideas to hand if someone asks you if you have any gift requests. At birthdays and Christmases, my mother always asks me if there is anything I need, and having a wish list helps both her and me. Otherwise, she will get me (in her words), 'something horrible', or my brother's term, 'knick-knacks

and cloggers'. Yes, my family does have fun together! I often feel greedy making a wish-list, but when you think about it, you don't want someone to waste their money buying you something you are never going to use. And equally, I would rather buy someone a gift they will appreciate and be excited about receiving.

44. **Be a library girl**. I have long been a public library user, ever since I was very young. These days I don't go into the actual building so much, because a lot of their material is online too. You can download eBooks to read on your Kindle, listen to eAudiobooks on your phone, and stream arthouse movies. There are even the latest eMagazines which are great to read on a tablet. All for free. You are already paying for these things indirectly through your property taxes (whether you rent or own), so you may as well make use of them. And it's so handy too!

45. **Remove negative words about money from your life**. Instead of 'I can't afford this', say 'I'm choosing not to buy this right now'. Just because it's not in your budget today doesn't mean it never will be. It feels far better to be discerning than feel poor. Likely you *can* afford that thing anyway, it's just that you choose not to buy it right now, or ever (discerning!) Make it seem like you have a

choice – because you do – both to yourself and others. Be sure in your decision, which all comes back to your values and what you prioritize.

46. **Surround yourself with people who have a positive mindset**. I do believe you can be a 'penny-pincher' in a chic, abundant, and luxurious way. It's all about how you sell something to yourself. I have known extremely broke people who you'd never know had very little money. One lady I knew wore bright red lipstick and was always upbeat and cheery. She dressed almost exclusively from thrift stores and was immaculate in her appearance. She had many interests and hobbies and had a lot of fun even though she was getting by on a miniscule income. I have also known wealthy people who were always crying poor. If you must be around such people, blind them with your shining light. Be yourself. Lead by example what it's like to have an inner confidence in your own situation.

47. **Keep your wallet and purse neat, clean, tidy and in good repair**. When I arrive back home from going out, I tip everything from my handbag onto my bed and put back the items I permanently keep in there – two reusable shopping bags tucked into their own pouches, my wallet, a small zip purse with lipstick, a tiny

handcream, perfume samples, a few headache tablets and a nail file etc, my sunglasses and car keys. Any carpark receipts go in the bin, and store receipts go into a basket to file. Creating this habit means your bag is always ready to go, and you feel the ease of a tidy handbag.

48. **Create your own spa experience**. One of my favourite rich girl habits is to have my spa time in the morning. I love showers rather than baths, so I have a nice, long shower where I wash my hair with my current favourite shampoo and conditioner, gently exfoliate my face, and buff my body with shower gel and a long-handled netting pouf. I really enjoy doing my back, it feels so good. After my shower I put SPF lotion on my face and décolletage, and a rich moisturizer on the rest of my body: feet, legs, stomach, arms and shoulders. I wear a cozy, fluffy robe and hotel slippers while it all soaks in. Some mornings when I have less time, I don't get to do everything I'd like to, but mostly I make this beautiful start to my day a priority. Perhaps you are a bath person. Perhaps you do this routine at night. Regular 'spa time' is a wonderful way to pamper yourself whichever way you do it.

49. **Look after your complexion**. You can have that rich girl glow and not spend a lot on skincare. I know, because I have done this for almost forty years. The only times when I have used expensive products was when I worked for Dior in their New Zealand office. Apart from that, 95% of the time I prefer supermarket and drugstore products. What does count though, is cleansing and moisturizing your face twice a day, every day. In the morning I use the tiniest amount of foaming cleanser along with warm water in the shower. I then apply eye cream and sun protective moisturizer. At night I use micellar water on a flat cotton pad to remove my makeup, then a few pumps of facial cleansing oil and a hot, wrung-out facecloth to remove. You can use any oil – almond, olive, or coconut. Then a night cream and eye cream. If I have a serum or facial oil, I'll put that on first. I started when I was 13, but if you still don't do this, the best time to begin is right now. You will see a difference quickly!

50. **Create a luxurious evening regime**. Instead of watching television or scrolling social media right up until the time you go to bed, devise a five-star night-time routine instead. Imagine what you would do if you were staying at a luxury retreat. There might be yoga stretching, hot herbal tea to sip, and a

relaxing massage booked. The room you are staying in is calm, and simply but beautifully furnished. How to do this for yourself though? Tidy up your bedroom and put any clothes or shoes away. Wash your face and apply a face mask. Do a few light stretches – whatever feels good. Make yourself a chamomile or peppermint tea and choose some reading material. Massage cream into your feet and put a pair of fluffy bed-socks on while it soaks in. Read your book while your face mask works, and sip your tea. You won't believe how soothed and ready for sleep you are as you snuggle into bed after removing your face mask and applying night cream. Sweet dreams!

51. **Develop a luxurious morning routine**. Morning routines are all the rage, and for good reason. A good start to the day sets you up for success, and if you have a morning routine to look forward to, you will be happy to get out of bed. I developed mine over a decade ago when I still worked in a full-time job, but now I work from home as a writer I still do the same routine because I love it so much. I get up at 6am, because I love rising early, and I start my day with a big mug of hot tea. Then, I either read and journal in bed, with all my pillows stacked up behind me, or I'll go straight to my office and write a chapter. I love writing early

in the morning; it's when I am freshest and the words just flow. After my writing time I'll either go for a walk on my treadmill or take the dogs for a long walk down the road, depending on the weather. Then it's smoothie time, make the bed, take a shower and get dressed, do my hair, makeup etc. The dogs have a walk if I haven't already taken them and often I'm up to lunchtime by then. But the basic start is the same most days, and I love it. You might have two morning routines, one for a workday and one for a weekend day. Consider how you best work in the morning. If you are a night owl you might like lots of time to get ready in the morning. I am a morning person, but I still like to start slowly. What is your ideal morning routine if you could design one? Journal on it and see if you can make it happen.

52. **Do nothing whenever you get the chance**. One of the most luxurious things I can think of is unstructured leisure time: When there is a day with no appointments or commitments. When you can rise when you want to and wake up slowly with a cup of tea. When you can start the day off reading a book. Maybe you'll never get a whole day like that (or could you?) but at least claim a few hours regularly to do exactly as you please. Gaze out the window. Contemplate life. Lie flat on your back and melt into the floor, stretching your

arms and legs out. The best luxury in the world is to have the feeling of endless time.

53. **Pretend that your life is a movie**. Some of my most productive and stylish days have been when I've created my own movie life. Imagining a camera is focused on you will have that effect, you will find. You will stand or sit up straighter, have lighter, more feminine hand movements and have a more pleasant look on your face. Because the camera is on! You might be in a movie about a young lady working in her job, or a perfect housewife pottering around making her home beautiful. Or perhaps you're starring in a movie about a woman who goes out with her friends. Look at the fun she is having. It all sounds silly, I know! But it's an entertaining way to feel like you're living your best life, and then, well, you end up living your best life, because you *are* that person. *Acting as if* leads to a luxe life!

54. **Simplify your home**. Mess and clutter are the opposite of abundance and luxury. Choose one area or category in your home and highly simplify it. If you don't want to donate or sell the extras but at the same time never seem to use them, store them away for a time, perhaps three or six months. Giving yourself this option will lessen the panicked feeling of getting rid of stuff you 'might need', but you

could surprise yourself when you are picking out your favourite items that you are happy to let the rest go. Then, move onto another area, and another. With each small section you complete, you will begin to feel lighter and happier. You would think luxury = more, but the reverse is true, as already illustrated in previous tips!

55. **Use what you have**. You might have certain categories where you habitually buy more before you use products up. One of mine is makeup; it's so easy to purchase a new lipstick, eyeliner or highlighting powder – when I already have multiples of these at home already! Because it feels better for me to be more minimal, I have now committed to using up all the lovely makeup I already own, because it doesn't last forever as you know. Since I started this, the only items I have had to replenish are mascara (about every 3-4 months), and foundation. It is so satisfying to use products right to the end – there is a lot of lipstick left in an 'empty' tube that you can use with a lip brush, and it gives a better result than applying it directly too. You will save money for when you do need something new and get your money's worth from what you have previously purchased. Plus, by using and enjoying what you own you are acknowledging the abundance you already have.

56. **Clean out storage areas** so you can put items away and out of sight but still access them easily. It feels luxurious to open a drawer or cupboard and have it be only half-full instead of overflowing. And having less on display in each room gives a pleasing, calm look; your eyes will be able to rest, and subconscious stress levels will lower. One example is the top of your nightstand. If yours is piled high with lip balm, eye drops, multiple books and journals, pens, tissues, and hand cream, clear out the top drawer and use that area instead. Then you will only have a few items by your bed such as a lamp and a book; it's far more peaceful to view this. Think about elegant hotels; everything you see is curated to a certain style. There is nothing superfluous, but everything is still to hand. *That* is luxury.

57. **Entertain at home**. When I was growing up, my parents were always throwing (and attending) dinner parties (and we lived in a normal neighbourhood, it's just what people did back then). Dinner parties seem to have died out for a while and in recent times I would more often meet friends at a restaurant. But your money goes far further when you dine at home, and it's a more relaxed atmosphere as well. You get to entertain in a very exclusive private dining room (yours!), and it's fun to set a beautiful table with your nicest dishes, cloth

dinner napkins, and candles galore. Curate a funky playlist on Spotify or get your old CDs out and set the scene to spoil your friends or family with. I love to do big Sunday lunches for family birthdays or special days such as Easter Sunday. My recommendation is to start off small (four or six people total) and work your way bigger if you want to.

58. **Perfect a few wow-factor recipes**. Think about what you would absolutely love to see on a menu if you were dining at a fine restaurant. Then, do a little research online, perhaps follow a YouTube video or two, and try making it for yourself. Recipes don't even need to be difficult to impress people and make a meal more special. I have always loved *Potatoes au Gratin* (also called *Gratin Dauphinoise*). I mean, who wouldn't when it includes ingredients such as potato, butter, cream, gruyere cheese and fresh herbs. Or perhaps you would like to be known as the girl who whips up a batch of Macarons with ease. With internet recipes now so accessible we have instant gratification at our fingertips.

59. **Have a signature cocktail**. I once went to a party at the home of an extremely wealthy couple. One of the fabulous details I remember from that evening was that there were jugs of Cosmopolitan cocktail which the waitstaff

circulated, topping peoples glasses up from. Yes, it was the early 2000s, but amazingly, the Cosmo has become almost a classic now. Imagine if you had a signature cocktail that you could put together in a few minutes. It might be a classic such as a martini, or perhaps something fashionable like a Negroni or Aperol Spritz. Espresso martinis are making a comeback too I've seen. Whatever yours is, have a few ingredients on hand to offer *your* signature cocktail to guests rather than saying, 'What would you like to drink?'

60. **Make music part of your life**. If I am at home, there is music playing. For such a small price, or free if you already own the CDs, you can create any atmosphere you like. I happily pay a monthly fee to use Spotify without advertisements, after I worked out it was less than the cost of one iTunes album per month. And the best part about Spotify, apart from the fact that I can play any song I want in an instant, is the fabulous endless array of playlists – music already curated for any occasion. 'Song radio' runs a close second. You choose a song, then go to that song's 'radio', and a whole playlist based on this song will come up. It's wonderful! During the day while I am working, I play tinkling piano music reminiscent of a hotel lobby (such as from Café BGMC, also on YouTube), switching to cool

Soho House vibes at happy hour, and jazz with dinner. Then, while I am relaxing before bed, my Dior Relaxing Music (saved under my name 'Fiona Ferris' on Spotify) is played. In my opinion, music is one of *the* top ways to live a luxurious life on a budget!

61. **Be a wonderful conversationalist**. You might notice that wealthy people are very good at conversing. Certainly the ones I know are. Maybe it's all those fancy functions they go to? Something they all have in common is that they listen, ask questions, and keep the conversation flowing with interesting (but not long-winded) stories, and are upbeat too. They have inspired me to be the same, after all, if you are invited somewhere it is part of your unspoken contract to be a charming participant. But it's for everyone's pleasure, yours included. Talk about books you have read, movies you've seen, local events coming up, and what you have been doing lately. Focus on the happy and the positive; you won't feel good about yourself afterwards if you get onto a complaining or venting topic. Ask me how I know that! And likewise, gossip never goes down well either. If you must talk about others say only nice things, and talk those people up.

62. **Request cosmetic samples**. When I worked at Parfums Christian Dior, we were always sending out packages of samples for the latest fragrance or beauty cream to our retailers. These would be kept behind the counter and given to customers who showed a genuine interest. So, next time you are in a department store or cosmetic emporium, ask the sales assistant if there are any new fragrance or beauty samples available. You will get to try the latest products for nothing, and maybe find a new favourite perfume too. Instead of saving these samples for trips (I never remembered to bring them along), use the face creams as a nice treat at night, and keep fragrance samples in your handbag to refresh you when you are out.

63. **Look around thrift stores**. I have long been a fan of charity stores and have found some fabulous bargains, including items I adore and still have to this day. It's like a treasure hunt because you never know what is going to turn up. You can buy wonderful old books that not only is the story a good read (and a chance to marvel at how society has changed), but they add a vintage touch to your bookshelves and tablescapes too. I have found beautiful candle glasses, and one particularly special French etched lithophane for only fifty cents. Because items are already used, you can add an instant

patina to your home style with well-chosen donated items, *and* you get to support a local charity too.

64. **Go to an art museum**. If you live in an area that has an art museum, lucky you. There is nothing like gazing up at stunning pieces of art to elevate the spirit. And isn't it fabulous that you don't even need to own these pieces to be able to enjoy them? It is impossible to feel poor when you are surrounded by beauty on such a grand scale, and you will find that you look at the world differently when you exit the gallery. It is a very inspiring and cultured way to spend an hour or two.

65. **Browse a well-to-do shopping area**. People watch and window shop. Dress as if you lived there. Buy a coffee and sit in a café with a real book (perhaps a well-thumbed volume of *The Great Gatsby*) or a notebook where you can write down your current inspiration and chic sightings. Feel the luxury in the air. Walk around and absorb the atmosphere while you observe people. How are they dressed? What differences do you notice? You don't need to spend anything to gain a great deal. As with visiting an art museum, I always come away feeling like a newer version of myself after an outing like this.

66. **Do your own manicure**. Polished nails = luxury lady. If mani-pedis are not in your budget, buy yourself a bottle of good quality nail polish and have a manicure at home. For a chic look go for classic red or plum, or soft, sheer pink. Don't be tempted by the cheapest polishes, I have found from experience they chip within the day. Revlon is one of my favourites for good quality at a reasonable price. And be sure to apply a clear topcoat too, this will preserve your manicure for longer. Try to have at least one professional manicure though, just so you can see how they do it and what the effect is like.

67. **Hydrate yourself with water**. A wealthy life is a healthy life. Water is pretty much free, so why not make the most of this incredible beauty elixir. Refill bottles to keep in your car and sip as you drive. I am always amazed when I get home with yet another empty water bottle. Sip, sip, sip all day and feel your cells glow with happiness. Water will help you keep slim, look younger and feel better. Instead of thinking, 'I *should* drink more water', imagine you're a Hollywood starlet sipping on her big bottle of water. Have you ever noticed celebrities are always lugging a giant bottle around? They know it's an important part of looking and feeling good.

68. **Listen to audiobooks while you do household tasks**. Maybe you don't have a housekeeper, butler or personal assistant (le sigh, wouldn't that be wonderful?), but everyday chores can become something to look forward to when you have an audiobook on the go. Your local library will have apps available to download titles to so you can listen via your phone whether you have Wi-Fi available or not. It's incredible the range of books available – both fiction and non-fiction, and always the latest releases. Doing meal prep and clearing out your fridge, putting away laundry, tidying the house; everything becomes lighter and more fun because you're listening to a good story while you do it. I either use a Bluetooth speaker if no-one else is home, or a pair of Air Pods and my phone in my back pocket if I am moving around the house.

69. **Eat real food**. Buy the fresh apple in preference to a packaged muesli bar. Stock less long-life food in your pantry and more fresh food in your fridge. Luxury and wealth go together with a healthy, vivacious body. You become what you eat, so do you want to become a devitalized, pale version of yourself, or would you rather work towards becoming someone who is vibrant and energized from a diet which includes zingy enzymes and water-rich foods? Make it easy and fun and

something to look forward to rather than a dreaded should-do. Wash and dry fresh herbs, and wash and slice containers of fruit and vegetables enough for the next few days. It will be easy and delicious to have fresh pineapple and peach with Greek yoghurt, sliced almonds and toasted coconut flakes for breakfast, or whip up a quick omelette with red bell pepper and fresh parsley for lunch. Doesn't that sound more luxurious and delicious than opening a plastic packet and shaking cereal into a bowl or unwrapping a paper-wrapped burger?

70. **Slow down your experience**. Instead of rushing, which can often be more of a habit rather than the actual need for speed, calm your nervous system by slowing *everything* down. Your pace, your speech, your reactions. Be intentional with your movements and precise in your actions. Don't waste energy on hurrying – be efficient and calm. Have you ever been around people who are flustered and bothered as a default way of being? It is so stressful! You might not be that extreme, but it is still a good practice to slow down so you can be present in your life. Enjoying our life every day is a luxury many of us pass up when we let ourselves be rushed. Choose a peaceful feeling of wellbeing instead. Be unhurried. Be in control of your time, and relax.

71. **Surround yourself with your own reminders of luxury**. Cleanliness, order, simplicity, fresh flowers, shiny gold or gilt touches, sumptuous textures such as velvet, big sunglasses, lip gloss, painted nails, hand cream, gold jewellery, classic colour combos, a simple outfit with wow-factor shoes, good posture, an elegant demeanour, a clean and tidy car, a regularly organized wallet, fresh fruit, water-rich foods, drinking water, sipping red wine slowly, finishing a meal with cheese, candles, music, time to read a good book, fresh air... these are all anchors for me and my version of a luxurious life. What belongs on your list?

72. **Be a savvy shopper**. Where brand doesn't matter for items such as simple white dishes, or a cozy robe for winter, buy inexpensively but with discernment for quality, looks and feel. And in situations where it is more important, buy the brand name or designer item. It's the high-low mix we've all heard about, but it applies to everything in your life, not just your outfit. Good quality furniture (not necessarily bought new) accessorized with inexpensive, thrifted, or homemade pillows. And when you do buy more expensive items, find the best price you can. It seems like basic common sense, but most people don't do this. A few minutes of research online can help

you save quite a bit of money, *often for exactly the same item.*

73. **Shop second-hand**. When you need a luxury goods fix, look online at sites such as eBay or Poshmark. We don't have either in New Zealand, so I use TradeMe (our version of eBay) for quicker postage. I have found some wonderful designer label goods at excellent prices simply from people having a big clear out and wanting things *gone*. Always do your due diligence to make sure you aren't just throwing your money away – look at the seller's feedback to make sure it's favourable, see how long they have had their account for, and how many transactions they have made.

74. **Have your home cleaned professionally**. You might think having a weekly cleaner is the most unnecessary and frivolous thing you could ever spend your cash on. And if that's true for you, excellent. But for me, it's the best money I spend all week, and it's part of the luxury lifestyle I desire for myself. It feels so abundant to have a sparkling clean home every Friday. I no longer procrastinate all day doing it myself, it's done and dusted (quite literally) in two hours. I have effortless motivation to do extra cleaning and tidying on top of the basics so that I feel like I'm living my dream life. I get to employ a lovely lady and help support her

family. You might be different; you might enjoy doing your own cleaning. But for me, there are other expenditures I'd happily replace to keep our cleaner *forever*. If you dread cleaning too, is there any way you can work into your budget someone for an hour a week, or once or twice a month?

75. **Make incremental upgrades**. Living a luxurious life on a budget isn't all about cutting back and going without. Part of it is growing what you are available for, such as my cleaner example above. Making slight changes is more comfortable for us mentally and being able to afford it financially too. You might have this shimmery mirage dream of living a fabulously luxurious life, however feel like it's a long way from where you are now. But you can make small upgrades as you come across them, and over time you will become closer to the lifestyle you would love to live. Every little thing counts, they all build on each other, and you will expand your capacity to receive as well. I started with tiny upgrades such as buying the thicker, softer tissues. I changed the milk I buy to one that I had previously deemed too expensive (when it was not that much more than the watery milk I used to buy). And the feeling of abundance I receive from these two modest examples alone? It is so worth it.

76. **Be an art collector**. Pictures from your childhood that you still love, thrifted prints and paintings, art from new artists, and creating your own with a stretched canvas or standard frame. There are so many savvy ways to collect art, and beautiful ways in which to display it as well. One tip that I have found excellent is to move your current art around: different walls, different rooms. Clean the glass and dust the frames as you do so. Each piece of art will look new and fresh when you change where it's hanging. Maybe even have an art swap with a family member or trusted friend if you have similar taste. You could agree on a set time, say six months.

77. **Create a gallery wall**. Whenever I see a display of cohesively grouped artwork it looks very 'designer', and I have always coveted this look for myself, so I set about creating my own. We have one wall in our living room where I've collected landscapes in oils framed in either gold or wood. A couple of them were gifts, and the rest I have collected inexpensively over the past few years. I also have a gallery wall above my writing desk. One picture is a screen-print from a young artist while I visited London and had framed when I arrived home, and the rest are, again, all inexpensively bought from charity stores and auctions. As with my living room gallery wall, they are similar in their

colours and themes (European scenes in soft-bright tones, framed in soft blue-greys and creams). You may already have prints that you can group together for a designer look instead of dotting them around.

78. **Live in your own fantasy world every day**. This is how you can create the world you want to inhabit. Decide that you get to live a luxurious life. Inhale that concept. Let it infuse into your very being. Fall in love with your life. View it through rose-tinted glasses. Be fanciful. Dance in your mind. Put into place all those pretty details that make you happy. People might look at you sideways, but only if you tell them your thoughts and inner motivations. Don't do that! Keep your beautiful and beguiling plans, dreams and ideas in your secret garden and let them wonder why you seem so happy and animated these days.

79. **Cultivate contentment**. There is a line between seeking out inspiration, and feeling 'less than' because you are comparing yourself with others. Learn to distinguish the two so you can continue on when you feel good or stop immediately and do something else if you find you are not feeling so high vibe. For example, some days you might love viewing others on social media or in magazines; seeing

how they live and style themselves. Other days this is not so helpful. Those are the days to immerse yourself in your own life, find contentment in the simple things, and tidy up loose ends.

80. **The feeling of luxury**. Identify what luxury *feels* like for you, so you can add more of it into your life. For me, luxury is soft textures, open space, free time, a relaxed and stress-free body, and that feeling of walking into a beautiful five-star hotel lobby, looking like a movie star, of course! It's also the feeling of having a breezy, open home with minimal tidying and cleaning to do because it's done all the time in an effortless way. Time for dreaming, time for sewing and knitting, time for watching movies and reading, time for writing, time for pottering and changing decorative items around. My luxury feels relaxed, comfortable, and convenient. What does *your* luxury feel like?

81. **Include all your senses.** Journal on how you can be luxurious on a sensual level. What does luxury *look* like for you? For me, it is a clear view of the sky, mature trees, a tidy and organized space, and a bookshelf filled with favourites old and new. What about *taste*? My luxurious tastes focus on clean and healthy foods that make my body feel light and elegant,

fresh flavours – seafood, fruit, and vegetables, and simple home-cooked meals. *Luxurious sound*? My list includes peace and quiet, classical music playing softly in a hotel lobby, low melodic voices, and jazz music in a winery tasting room. And finally, *scent*. Luxury for me smells like a florist's shop, freshly brewed coffee, and scented body products – soap, body creams, lotions and perfume, and letting the fresh air in by having windows open. Spend some time with your journal and go through all five senses to bring more luxury into your life in many small ways.

82. **Tidy your environment with mini projects**. Choose an area that is currently bothering you. It might be your bedroom, your car, your nightstand, your closet, or a drawer or cupboard. Right now, I'm thinking of my pantry. I tidy it every so often and haven't done so in a while. But I know when I do give it a spruce-up I feel amazing and more focused on healthful eating. If I was to makeover my pantry, I would empty everything out onto the kitchen counter and wipe down all the shelves. Then I would scrutinize each item to make sure it is within date as I put things back neatly. If some are close to expiry, I would make plans to use them in a meal. It feels so good to open a neat and clean pantry.

83. **Have a spa retreat day**. Imagine on a day off from work when you have no special plans, to designate that your spa day. Imagine taking the whole day for yourself to relax and rejuvenate. What kinds of things could you do? I would recommend doing a very quick tidy of the house, so it is an environment of peace, luxury and calm, but after that, the day is all yours. How about a yoga or stretching session, a walk outside in nature, quiet time to read, diffusing essential oils, doing a guided meditation, preparing simple meals, and taking a day off from all screens. Doesn't this sound like a wonderfully restorative day?

84. **Create a truly luxurious lifestyle**. What really matters in life aren't expensive items and fancy gadgets. When you think about it, wellbeing, deep inner peace, comfort, simple happiness, order, quiet time, kindness, the need for good sleep, nutrition, something to occupy the mind, purposeful action, beauty, harmony and spaciousness are all far more luxurious. Keep these words in mind next time your mind is racing, or you are feeling caught up in the outside world, for good or bad. Yes, we can enjoy our own favourite comforts and luxury goods, but a foundation of peace will keep us grounded.

85. **Live in the present moment**. Remember that you never have to 'do' anything, you can just 'be'. Enjoy your wonderful life. Let people be who they are. Forget about yesterday and tomorrow. Today is where it's at. Notice how your body feels. Listen for the sounds around you. Practice dropping into the present moment often. Dwell there. Defocus your eyes as you gaze at a long view and breathe deeply. Luxuriate in presence. Give it to yourself. Give it to others. Listen, observe, absorb. Focus on doing one thing at a time. Feel your nervous system unwind, your blood pressure drop. Relax.

86. **Live the rich lady life**. Designate yourself the rich lady, even if your income isn't so rich. Claim richness in *all* areas of your life. Reframe *everything*. Don't just go for a walk because you should be healthier. Go for a walk with your big sunglasses on and stride it out – you are a fabulously wealthy heiress exercising in Central Park. Your yoga and stretching in front of YouTube isn't just so you won't be creaky when you get older. You are having a private lesson in your own home. Create a rich lady backdrop to everything you do for the ultimate in fun inspiration.

87. **Have tissues in every room**. Choose the thickest, softest tissues you can find, and place them in each room – find the prettiest boxes you can. For only a few dollars per box, and they'll last for ages, you can feel like you are in a luxury hotel where your every move is anticipated. I copied this from noticing how our favourite five-star hotel did the same thing, and it really does feel luxurious for a tiny financial outlay. Even my husband said that he loves whenever he needs a tissue, there is one right there. You can find inexpensive, attractive tissue box covers too, or make your own if you are handy with a sewing machine.

88. **Create your own magazines**. Recently when we went away on a two-night mini-break, I had the thought to buy a thick, glossy magazine for a treat. I used to *love* magazines and bought too many. They were my happy place! But then I remembered that magazines aren't as inspiring to me as they used to be. So I decided to create my own, with inexpensive display binders (books with clear plastic sleeves), favourite torn-out pages from magazines, and articles and blog posts I've printed out over the years. They are so fun to browse through and really scratch my magazine itch. If you miss magazines from your youth as well, why not put together your own?

89. **Make your own rules**. One of the most luxurious things you can do is be able to live life on your own terms. All of us will have restrictions of some kind – financial, time, family obligations. But we can still put our own preferences into place to have us feel like we have a choice. Like we are the ones in charge of our own lives. And, you get to break your own rules or reset them at any time you like. You are always free to change your mind. Ask yourself if you are really living your life on your own terms. You might not love your job, but you love earning money, so you could say you are there by choice. And it's a wonderful goal to be able to get there one day and say that yes, you are living your life completely on your own terms. By the way, what *are* your terms?

90. **Upgrade your sleepwear**. Can you imagine your favourite glamorous movie star going to bed in a stretched out old tee-shirt? I don't think so. How about a satin cami set or pretty slip? Much better. For minimal expenditure (there are some lovely nightwear options around at excellent prices) you can go to bed feeling like a total bombshell diva. And while you're at it, get the satin robe too. There is nothing like the feeling of silky, floaty fabric to impart a feeling of luxury. Satin is easy to care for, it's a total wash-and-wear fabric which dries in a flash. And it's very comfortable to

wear in bed too; turning over is easier since the material is quite slippery, and your nightwear won't bunch up!

91. **Become financially savvy**. Educate yourself with books that resonate. Find someone who speaks in a way you understand and learn more about money management. Keep your study simple and don't let overwhelm get you. Read the financial pages; you might not understand everything, I certainly don't, but you will always learn something. Even if you don't have much money to spare, you can still start an investment. The index fund I contribute to requires $50 per month as a minimum. You might find one that needs even less. You can then feel like you're 'in the market' because you are. It is *so* empowering to know even a little bit about personal finance.

92. **Tour beautiful homes**. If there are fund-raising home tours in your area, *go on them*. I have done a couple and spent the day viewing lovely homes. It sounds like a funny thing to do, but gosh, after that day I felt in a different mindset. I was keen to go home and make *my* home look better. I was inspired to tidy up even more and plant brightly coloured flowers in outdoor pots. Seeing how taken care of these homes were was so uplifting, and of course it's

always fun to see inside the fancy places. My personal standards were raised instantly. Or, if you have open homes for sale, why not go for a look? Real estate agents *want* people to go through a home when it is open for a public viewing. Even if you are not in a position to buy, it makes the listing look more popular which they love. If you dress nicely and are respectful there is no harm.

93. **Declutter anything that does not feel high vibe**. There is no rule that says you must keep everything forever. If you have photos of yourself and you remember that day as not being so good, or you look far worse than you see yourself in your head, throw them out. If you feel guilty looking at a gift you were given that is *so* not your style, donate it. If you avoid certain clothes that while technically are fine but you never feel good in them, donate them too. You will find with these micro-actions that each low-vibe item you remove from your life will leave you feeling lighter, luckier, happier, and more like you are living your luxurious life. Of anything you are dithering about, ask yourself, 'Is this high vibe enough for me?', 'Is it Me 2.0?', or 'Is it good enough for the future vision I have for myself?' You should receive a clear answer.

94. **Be 'boutique'.** Keep the vision in mind that your closet, and indeed your home, be a small and exclusive boutique of curated beauty (in preference to an over-stocked bargain warehouse). And you, it's elegant proprietor. When you keep the boutique idea front-of-mind for your wardrobe, or boutique hotel for your home, it makes decisions easier. Decisions such as, 'Shall I get rid of this?', 'Shall I wash my hair today or go the dry shampoo again?', or 'Shall I go for a walk outside or zone out with my phone on the sofa?' It's always a good idea to keep a decent stash of motivational tricks in your chic toolbox, and the boutique vision is an excellent one!

95. **Create your own dupes.** Just as in the makeup world, you can find a dupe for any item you covet but don't want to pay a high price for. I love Aerin Lauder's polished Park Avenue look both in her personal and her home style. However, her products are *très* expensive! I have her two books and some of her fragrances, but for the rest I look at how she creates her aesthetic and borrow from the parts I like. It's the same with Ralph Lauren's English country home style. His goods are so pricey, especially here where I live in New Zealand. So, I am inspired by his 'essence' instead, and display homemade tartan pillow

covers mixed in with small actual Ralph Lauren merchandise items such as elegant cloth dinner napkins, and a beautiful enamel tray which I have hung on the wall as an art piece. Whatever your favoured design style is, mix real with 'in the style of' and create your own unique look.

96. **Strike a balance between staying in and going out**. My father used to say that you put your hand in your pocket as soon as you leave the house. And it's true, it is basically free to stay at home. But we need a balance of both. I adore devising my own experience at home, such as having a simplified, decluttered home that feels luxurious in its spaciousness. And I also love to dress up and go out, whether it's for errands or to lunch. The key is to find things you enjoy doing that don't necessarily cost a lot of money. Look for the value in everything you purchase. Life is short, go out and have fun, but also be slickly savvy with your spending. Be that wealthy older person in retirement who made wise spending decisions when younger.

97. **Cultivate luxurious habits**. Brainstorm or research a lusciously long list of indulgent habits that you'd love to incorporate into your daily life. Refer to this list and choose from it often so you can truly feel like you are living

your most luxurious life. Bonus points if they cost nothing! Here are some of mine to get you started: Practising exquisite self-care, making a fruit-filled mocktail to sip in hot weather or a hot drink with whipped cream on top in the winter, full-body moisturization after a shower, relaxing journaling and inspiration time before bed, re-reading favourite books, a coffee date with friends, movie afternoons on a Sunday whether at home or out, getting a massage, doing my nails or having them done. Whatever feels luxurious and special to you, write it down and start cultivating your luxurious habits today.

98. **Create your future with your imagination**. I adore this quote from Estee Lauder which says, *"Make the most of what you have. If you can't have everything you think you deserve at that moment, you would do well to surround yourself with symbols of your ideals. I surrounded myself with touches of the good life; the lovely and intricately tapestried life of my imagination, an imagination that has always been, I'm proud to say, large enough to admit any possibility."* Why *wouldn't* you want to start small and dream big? Have expansive desires for the future and begin where you are right now. Surround yourself with small reminders in

your immediate environment and anchor in that feeling of luxury and beauty.

99. **Be self-motivated**. Luxury isn't lazy. Luxury might like relaxation, but she relaxes with intention. She is not lying around on the sofa flicking between channels. She is someone who loves life. She bounces out of bed in the morning because she ate and drank in moderation the evening before and got a good night's sleep. She exercises in a happy state of mind and enjoys the feeling of a flexible body. She joyfully eats foods that she knows sit well in her stomach. She does her work *and* takes time to relax. Creating your own version of a luxury lifestyle takes work, but it's fun work. What better thing is there to build than your dream life? Coming at your goals from this angle will have you be excited to get going. There is no 'pushing yourself' needed, you will be pulled effortlessly along! Such fun!

100. **Own yourself**. It is wonderful to seek inspiration via new ideas and other people, but there is also great luxury to be had by simply loving yourself and loving who you are. Both can co-exist, and it's the sweetest spot to be in when you adore your life and yourself *and* are excited to create even more. More happiness, more fun style, more simplicity and more elegance. Own your personality, own your

quirks, even own the parts of yourself that are 'too much'. These are the aspects that make you 'you'. Owning yourself also brings a peaceful sense of empowerment too, because there is nothing inside you that others can trigger. You own the good parts and the bad and know that there is no need to be perfect. You do your best, you enjoy life, you love others and yourself, and that's all that is really needed for a happy and successful life!

And to finish, just for fun, to thank you for reading through this mini-book, I leave you with fifty extra bonus tips and reminders on how to live a luxurious life without spending a lot of money. Here's to you and your fabulous life!

50 bonus tips for living a fabulous life without spending a lot of money

1. Don't be afraid to be the best dressed person you know.

2. Learn to be fifteen minutes early for everything.

3. Talk much less than you currently do.

4. Write down in a notebook all the good ideas you come across for ongoing inspiration.

5. Tidy your home environment often and make it nice, as if visitors were coming over.

6. Practice taking pleasure in every moment of your day.

7. Only stock foods in your home that you picture yourself eating in your ideal healthy and luxe lifestyle.

8. Create space in your schedule to relax and do whatever you want.

9. Keep chores and admin up to date so you don't have jobs hanging over you.

10. Minimize possessions so you have less to look after.

11. Hire a cleaner, if not regularly, at least a one-off every now and then.

12. Stretch your body for five minutes a day.

13. Buy yourself a Vacu Vin wine saver so you can pour yourself a beautiful glass of wine to have with dinner and then seal the rest away for tomorrow.

14. Decide for yourself that you will only drink with a meal.

15. Feel fresh and new by listening to different music than usual, wearing different clothing combinations, or trying a different makeup look.

16. Apply self-tanner lightly on your arms and décolletage, and bronzing powder on your face when it's cold for that rich girl travel glow.

17. Buy a long-handled body brush to lather up in the shower and be able to reach everywhere, even your back.

18. Own your space in the world and be confident in who you are. There is no-one else like you!

19. Play elegant background music at a low volume when you are at home.

20. Declutter anything that makes you feel poor, broke or inconvenienced.

21. Use your good things every day.

22. Add fresh produce to each meal, no matter what you are having. A petite side salad with your lunch, a sliced pear after dinner.

23. Give each room in your home a thorough clean and tidy.

24. Use up consumable items before you replace them if you habitually over-purchase. We all have those categories!

25. Keep your car tidy and clean so that you'd be fine if anyone needed a lift somewhere at the last minute.

26. Upgrade your palate and become a food snob.

27. Visit an art gallery.

28. Learn about wine tasting.

29. Throw out any undies that qualify as 'sad' and buy yourself some new pairs if you don't have many left!

30. File your nails weekly so they are neat and all the same length. Either buff or apply polish. Push your cuticles back and nourish your nails with oil or cuticle cream.

31. Empty out your handbag and wallet daily, and remove receipts and anything that doesn't need to be in there.

32. Moisturize all over, every day, after your bath or shower.

33. Cut way, way back on sugar. You don't need a strict diet or a thirty-day cleanse, just pay attention to how much sugar is in your diet.

34. Look after your wardrobe. Make sure your clothes are clean, in good order and ready to go.

35. Collate a 'happy basket' for relaxing time, filled with items such as your journal and pen, reading glasses, the current book you are reading, hand cream, a needlepoint project, inspirational material, or whatever you love to have near you.

36. If your fridge, freezer and pantry are too full and you have to throw out expired foods regularly, commit to eating through your inventory and only buying the bare minimum of what you need

when grocery shopping. Have a fridge that you wouldn't dread someone opening!

37. Decide on your ideal hair-wash schedule and stick to it. Buy some dry shampoo and use sparingly.

38. Elevate your makeup game. Watch YouTube videos, and practice new looks. Notice characters in movies – how does their makeup look?

39. Drink lots of water, the ultimate – free – rich-girl habit.

40. Host a ladies afternoon tea on a Saturday and enjoy a couple of hours of relaxed, fun company. It feels so good to get together and have a laugh and a chat with a group of women, even if there are only a few of you.

41. Have exquisite posture. Feel an invisible string from the crown of your head pull you up effortlessly.

42. Eat at a beautifully set table, even on an ordinary night, in preference to the sofa and television. Light a candle. Put the good placemats and napkins out.

43. Give yourself a facial at home once a week. Plan for the night before you are going to wash your hair.

44. Spend less time looking at a screen and more time face-to-face.

45. Relax for an hour or so before bed with an inspiring book, soft instrumental music, and some quiet time.

46. Stop watching the news. You will still find out the important things to know.

47. Don't join in complaint-fests if you find yourself near one, and don't bring up complaints yourself.

48. Design a 21-piece collection for the month using clothing you already own.

49. Add a little more gold into your life – gold jewellery (costume or real), a gold edged phone cover or key ring, choosing gold hardware on a bag in preference to silver. There are so many inexpensive gold touches that give an aura of luxury.

50. Create your own fantasy dream world in your head and go about furnishing your real life with the details, piece by piece, and day by day.

To finish

And there you have it! Now it's up to you to carry on. To continue to look for all those little ways in which you can live well every day, and also how you can make life more fun, and easier on yourself.

When it comes to creating your most luxurious daily experience, the most important thing is that you take extra care and attention to the details of your life, making everything as lovely as you can. You get to choose *you* and how you want things to be – in great detail! You get to live a luxurious life in big ways and small, and *love* how you do it. You get to put into action every day all those little touches that make you happy.

You look at the bright side of life and love the sunshine it provides you with. You love the flavour of luxury you have chosen for yourself. You design your own collection of tastes, a bespoke blend that suits you perfectly. What could be more fabulous than that?

I sincerely hope you enjoyed this petite read and found it motivating in a fun and light way. I trust you will feel inspired to create small and luxurious changes in your life, for the better! Others will notice you are different, how can they not?

If you enjoyed this book, please would you take a minute to leave a brief review on Amazon? I would be so grateful for even a few words. A review is the biggest gift you can give me as it helps other lovely readers find my books too.

I wish you all the best and I look forward to seeing you in my next book!

Fiona

About the Author

Fiona Ferris is passionate about the topic of living well, in particular that a simple and beautiful life can be achieved without spending a lot of money.

Her books are published in five languages currently: English, Spanish, Russian, Lithuanian and Vietnamese. She also runs an online home study program for aspiring non-fiction authors.

Fiona lives in the beautiful and sunny wine region of Hawke's Bay, New Zealand, with her husband, Paul, their rescue cat Nina, rescue dogs Daphne and Chloe, and their cousin Micky dog.

To learn more about Fiona, you can connect with her at:
howtobechic.com
fionaferris.com
facebook.com/fionaferrisauthor
twitter.com/fiona_ferris
instagram.com/fionaferrisnz
youtube.com/fionaferris

Fiona's other books are listed on the next page, and you can also find them at:
amazon.com/author/fionaferris

Other books by Fiona Ferris

Thirty Chic Days: *Practical inspiration for a beautiful life*

Thirty More Chic Days: *Creating an inspired mindset for a magical life*

Thirty Chic Days Vol. 3: *Nurturing a happy relationship, staying youthful, being your best self, and having a ton of fun at the same time*

Thirty Slim Days: *Create your slender and healthy life in a fun and enjoyable way*

Financially Chic: *Live a luxurious life on a budget, learn to love managing money, and grow your wealth*

How to be Chic in the Winter: *Living slim, happy and stylish during the cold season*

How to be Chic in the Summer: *Living well, keeping your cool and dressing stylishly when it's warm outside*

A Chic and Simple Christmas: *Celebrate the holiday season with ease and grace*

The Original 30 Chic Days Blog Series: *Be inspired by the online series that started it all*

30 Chic Days at Home: *Self-care tips for when you have to stay at home, or any other time when life is challenging*

30 Chic Days at Home Vol. 2: *Creating a serene spa-like ambience in your home for soothing peace and relaxation*

The Chic Author: *Create your dream career and lifestyle, writing and self-publishing non-fiction books*

The Chic Closet: *Inspired ideas to develop your personal style, fall in love with your wardrobe, and bring back the joy in dressing yourself*

The Peaceful Life: *Slowing down, choosing happiness, nurturing your feminine self, and finding sanctuary in your home*

Loving Your Epic Small Life: *Thriving in your own style, being happy at home, and the art of exquisite self-care*

The Glam Life: *Uplevel everything in a fun way using glamour as your filter to the world*

100 Ways *to Live a Luxurious Life on a Budget*

100 Ways *to Declutter Your Home*

100 Ways *to Live a European Inspired Life*

100 Ways *to Enjoy Self-Care for Gentle Wellbeing and a Healthy Body Image*

100 Ways *to be That Girl*

100 Ways *to Be a Chic Success and Create Your Dream Life*

Printed in Great Britain
by Amazon